SIX STEPS FOR MANAGING LOSS

1

Other Titles by Father Curley:

Console One Another: A Guide to Christian Funerals. Sheed & Ward, Kansas City, MO, 1993.

The Ministry of Consolation: A Parish Guide for Comforting the Bereaved. Alba House, New York, 1993.

Healing the Broken-Hearted: Consoling the Grief-Stricken. Alba House, New York, 1995.

A Way of the Cross for the Bereaved. Alba House, New York, 1996.

Journey to Healing: A Ministry for the Bereaved. (Video) Alba House Communications, Canfield, OH, 1995.

SIX STEPS FOR MANAGING LOSS

A Catholic Guide Through Grief

TERENCE P. CURLEY, D.MIN.

ALBA·HOUSE   NEW·YORK

SOCIETY OF ST. PAUL, 2187 VICTORY BLVD., STATEN ISLAND, NEW YORK 10314

ST PAULS

Library of Congress Cataloging-in-Publication Data

Curley, Terence P., 1944-
    Six steps for managing loss: a Catholic guide through grief /
Terence P. Curley.
        p.   cm.
    Includes bibliographical references.
    ISBN 0-8189-0801-7
    1. Bereavement — Religious aspects — Catholic Church. 2. Grief —
Religious aspects — Catholic Church.   I. Title.
    BX2373.B47C87   1998
    248.8'66 — DC21   97-18065
                                                 CIP

Produced and designed in the United States of America by the
Fathers and Brothers of the Society of St. Paul,
2187 Victory Boulevard, Staten Island, New York 10314,
as part of their communications apostolate.

ISBN: 0-8189-0801-7

Printing Information:

Current Printing - first digit   1   2   3   4   5   6   7   8   9   10

Year of Current Printing - first year shown

1997   1998   1999   2000   2001   2002   2003   2004   2005

Dedication

With deep gratitude to my brother
Jerome M. Curley
for his original insights, editing and support
for the grief-stricken.

Table of Contents

Part I: Steps For Managing Loss 1

Introduction: Taking the Journey with Healing Steps 2

Step One: Acknowledge that we are powerless over the causes of loss, that grief happens, and that our lives can become unmanageable at times. 4

Step Two: Affirm that a Power greater than we can restore our balance. 13

Step Three: Freely turn ourselves toward God and let God take charge of our lives and healing. 19

Step Four: Examine our relationships and attachments to better understand ourselves and what is happening. 22

Step Five: Learn to love and trust again. Form a new spiritual relationship with the loved one who has died. 28

Step Six: Having experienced healing and having our loved ones restored to us in the ways of the Spirit, bring that message of life beyond death to others who are suffering. 31

Part II: Personal Prayer Guide 33
Prayers During Bereavement 33

Prayer Experience One: When Loss Happens 35
Psalm 130 35

Prayer Experience Two: Guidance Through Grief 37
Psalm 23: The Lord Is My Shepherd 37

Prayer Experience Three: "Feelings of Abandonment" 40
Psalm 22:1-6 40

Prayer Experience Four: "When Grief Is Longing and Yearning" 42
    Psalm 42:16 42

Prayer Experience Five: "When we need relief from grief" 45
    Psalm 13 45

Prayer Experience Six: Acceptance 47

Bibliographical References & Pastoral Topics 49

SIX STEPS FOR MANAGING LOSS

PART I

Steps For Managing Loss

1. Acknowledge that we are powerless over the causes of loss, that grief happens, and that our lives can become unmanageable at times.
2. Affirm that a Power greater than we can restore our balance.
3. Freely turn ourselves toward God and let God take charge of our lives and healing.
4. Examine our relationships and attachments to better understand ourselves and what is happening.
5. Learn to love and trust again. Form a new spiritual relationship with the loved one who has died.
6. Having experienced healing and having our loved ones restored to us in the ways of the Spirit, bring that message of life beyond death to others who are suffering.

INTRODUCTION

Taking the Journey with Healing Steps

People usually express good will when they hear about a loss. They extend sympathy and genuinely feel sorry about what has happened. Very often they try to help the bereaved. Help is expressed by a kind word, gesture, and advice. Advice may be given in a well-intentioned but nevertheless clichéd sort of way. Certain phrases have been tailored for the bereaved. "You have to let go." "It will pass with time." "You are strong enough to take it." These phrases often do more harm than good. The bereaved is left with a remark which really does not help one who is going through the process of grief. Often a remark becomes more of a hindrance, making people feel that their true feelings are not being noticed or appreciated in an adequate or appropriate way.

The steps outlined in this little booklet are not hard and fast rules. People go through the various stages of grief in ways that differ from individual to individual. The steps are merely a suggested framework to assist you according to your own needs, imagination and creativity. When circumstances force us to "let go" of our attachments we look for props to help us to do this. We need to know how others have managed to work through their grief and emerge both wiser and stronger as a result. Just as our relationships with our children change depending on their ages so, too, do our relationships with those who have died need to be redefined.

A step program such as this is designed to assist in dealing with life's attachments to which we have become, in a sense, addicted. For the most part when we think of a step program, we think of the treatment of addictions due to chemical dependency, e.g., alcohol and drugs. The overwhelming suffocation of grief can be likened to an addiction in that it, too, immobilizes all thoughts not related to the subject of our loss. We become obsessed with the absence of our loved one and our behavior depicts many of the characteristics we associate with addiction. Our lives are often literally shattered when grief is intense and sudden. We need to do something to manage rather than be managed by our loss.

There are many ways to use this guide. It can be a very helpful resource for small groups or be used by individuals who may want to keep a journal of their progress. The content may be applied to workshops or be a reflective tool for personal meditation and growth.

It is recommended that if you are using this guide as an individual you consider asking a friend to read it also. By having a compassionate friend able and willing to discuss your loss, healing may occur much faster. Hearkening back to the step model, a compassionate friend can act as a mentor during your time of grief. Being there for you, he or she will provide a sounding board for those thoughts and feelings you so often find difficult to express.

The steps are a framework for identifying and expressing your innermost feelings. They can, as steps, be taken according to your needs. They do not have to follow in sequence. Some times we may want to focus on a particular step which we believe is characteristic of our own personal grief at this specific moment. Grief is intensely personal and we bring to our losses our personal histories. The steps are to assist us with life's journey at a most difficult time.

STEP ONE

Acknowledge that we are powerless over the causes of loss, that grief happens, and that our lives can become unmanageable at times.

Independence is something we all prize. This is one of our earliest accomplishments. In childhood we cherish being able to control our lives. The more autonomous the better we feel about ourselves. Certainly this is encouraged as part of our learning experiences. When we believe that we can do everything and everything is possible, what happens when the bottom falls out of our plans?

Even though we have a sense of "limitlessness" the fact of the matter is we are "limited." In all of our lives we exclude far more than we include. Provisions are not made in our psyche for life's separations and losses. We hardly allow ourselves to anticipate what life will be like for us when a death occurs.

Powerlessness takes many forms. When we experience a loss there is shock. This occurs when there is an intense grief reaction. Intense grief can be expected whenever there is a significant bond with the deceased. Less intense grief reactions are more frequently present when there is not such significant bonding. For the most part the steps covered here are concerned with intense grief reactions.

Along with shock there may be a feeling of emptiness. It is as if the wind has been taken from our sails. Physical symptoms such as having difficulty in breathing (hyperventilation) can be present. We feel absolutely powerless and there is nothing we can do to change the situation. Denial or avoidance are ways in which we seek to regain some control over our lives once again.

Pastoral Examples

Shortly after Mary's husband died I received a call from a funeral director. He told me that the widow was making arrangements for her husband's funeral. She seemed to be doing pretty well but the funeral director felt that someone ought to talk with her.

When I arrived Mary was pretty self-possessed. She was a little tearful but cordial. While we spoke she started to sigh and I could see that she was having difficulty following the conversation. Mary's breathing became more labored. Then, she put her finger to her lips telling me to be quiet. I realized that every time I mentioned her husband's name she made this gesture for silence. She was in denial, refusing to admit or to accept or even to allow mention of the fact that her husband had died.

At the time of a death there are many gestures which manifest this sense of powerlessness or provide the first faint signs that we are beginning to manage our loss. The first few hours are critical for the way we go through grief. Very often, if we find ourselves in denial, we may find it helpful and even necessary to relive the critical event with someone we know will understand. The sense of powerlessness can be so overwhelming at the time, though, that later grief work may have to be done.

Another pastoral example is Ellen, who was married for forty-five years to her husband when he died very suddenly. She was numb during the funeral. Later during some support group sessions she admitted that there were whole portions of time she could not recall. There were people she met whom she thought she must have met somewhere else.

Abandonment & Attachments

Another significant symptom that is associated with powerlessness is the feeling of abandonment. We cry out: "How could you leave me like this?" "I want him back." "I can't let her go."

Detaching ourselves or letting go cannot happen in a vacuum.

There has to be some content or context for us to rely on in order to make the necessary adjustment. This step program addresses our belief system and what this specific relationship has come to mean in our lives. Grief is a highly personal experience.

A sense of abandonment is a very common reaction to what we perceive to be a loss. Our background, health, compulsions, and how we have dealt with loss in the past shape how we handle present disappointment. Our beliefs and hopes contribute enormously to our perception of what is happening to us. We realize when we delve into grief that a powerful personal faith inventory is often a necessity.

Mourning differs from grief. It is the public or cultural expression of loss. When we grieve with others, mourning occurs through various rituals. These rituals are very much the shared experience of whatever ethnic, racial, or religious background we share with others. As such the rituals influence the outcome of our grief. The rituals also determine appropriate and inappropriate reactions to our loss.

When we feel powerless there is a need to do something about it. We cannot passively coast through a critical event. Such detachment is not only inhuman but is detrimental to our health. Expression of emotions is necessary if we are to once again have balance. News of the death of someone near and dear to us is an assault to our personal health which needs to be dealt with. None of us can put our emotions on hold. When we do this the price we pay is far too high.

A healthy response requires the release of our feelings. Fortunately this is beginning to be seen as appropriate for males as well as females in our culture. There is no disgrace for a man to show the depth of his feelings by shedding tears, even publicly.

When we look at powerlessness as a major symptom of grief we are addressing how well we accept or deny a loss. Once we find ourselves willing to face the loss we have to, in our step program, admit that we really had not accepted what happened. Our minds play subtle and not so subtle tricks on us. We can easily deceive ourselves in the face of powerlessness. It is little wonder that people in denial say: "She has only gone away on a trip." "He's at school right now but he'll be home for the holidays." Sometimes false refuge is taken by retreating into what our conscious mind knows is really not true.

We must do grief work which in itself is no easy task. It is emotionally draining to make a commitment to face our losses. It requires courage and companionship. We really need both if we are to travel through the darkness of grief with hope for the dawn of a new life without our loved one on earth.

We know full well the feeling of powerlessness and its effects. What we have to work on is the management of our feelings at this critical time.

Step One Healing Tasks

1. Accept that you are powerless to change ultimate events and situations.
2. Express how you feel with a trusted friend or relative.
3. Explore ways to ritualize the loss. Join a support group, start a scholarship fund, keep a journal.
4. Be patient with yourself and your emotions.
5. Be patient with family members and friends.
6. Seek help in doing important tasks of grief work such as putting away the deceased person's belongings, concluding insurance matters, and taking care of other financial concerns.
7. Move into the mystical dimension by deciding how to best redefine your relationship with the deceased in a spiritual way.
8. Promise yourself that you will work at going through grief. (This may mean developing some creative responses to these steps.)
9. Always keep in mind that you have to manage your grief rather than let it manage you.
10. Permit yourself time to express your deepest feelings. Don't be alarmed every time you cry. It does not mean that you are returning to square one.

The Grief Process

Before we move on to the next step it is important that we have some information about the process of going through grief. This information will help us to recognize the common characteristics of grief that can be applied to our own personal situation.

Theories of Grief

There is no comprehensive theory on how to manage grief. What works for some others deplore. What is culturally acceptable varies from one ethnic group to another and from one nation to another. Even what society thinks is psychologically healthy is subject to varying opinions. We have to be able to move from a few general principles to specific applications tailored to our own situation. After all we are all unique and so are our relationships.

There are some phases peculiar to grief which seem to be more or less universal, however, and some approaches to managing it which seem to be held in common. When we put grief into perspective we are better able to manage it.

Shock and Numbness

Shock and numbness describes the first phase of intense grief. Eric Lindemann and other innovators of crisis theories initially placed the time of shock to be six to eight weeks. There is really no set time limit. Circumstances and relationships cause variables which are different in everyone's life. Generally we can look at approximately two months.

We can practice denial in a variety of ways. Recall the woman I talked with at the funeral home. Her way of denial was to gesture for silence when her husband's death was mentioned. She was shocked and totally unready to accept his death.

Yearning and Searching

Another phase after the initial period of numbness is that of yearning and searching. This is the time when in your bereavement, you try to keep as vivid as possible your memory of the deceased. All of the symptoms of loss ranging from restlessness and irritability to anger and frustration point toward your need to express your feeling of emptiness. It often expresses itself in an unresolved "searching" and "longing" for the "lost" loved one. This can be an extremely frustrating enterprise for anyone suffering from a loss. Considerable energy can be expended in the futile search to recapture some part of your life which is missing. This phase of searching has to be channeled by creative responses which will heal. This is the area where rituals for separation and loss can be so important.

Withdrawing

Once the searching and longing to be with the deceased loved one has ended another phase may occur. Disorganization and despair describe the mood of the bereaved person who has abandoned searching. Not only has the deceased's life ended but, as far as many of the bereaved are concerned, their life, too, has ceased. This is a time of deep depression which can become seriously debilitating if it goes unchecked. There is a tendency to turn in on oneself and to be preoccupied with one's own feelings. At this point in our step program, we recognize just how unmanageable our lives have become as a result of our continuing attachment to our deceased loved one.

Reorganization

Finally there is the phase of reorganization. This is the time of reinvesting in the future and relationships. We begin to see that we want to love again despite the risks. We begin to cultivate a renewed interest in life. Physically we feel better and have a clearer awareness of what is happening around us. Balance in body, mind and spirit is restored. This does not mean that the grieving process has ended. It simply means that the critical period is taking on a new shape. There is no time limit for grief. We have to learn to live with our losses.

Passages

A helpful explanation of the grief process is provided by the famous nineteenth century anthropologist Arnold Van Gennep. He devised the phrase "rites of passage" to describe the various phases that we have to go through in our ritualizing of loss. He tells us, for example, that it is necessary to (1) separate ourselves from our former state or status; (2) that we must go through a period of transition into a new state or status; and (3) we must incorporate ourselves into this new reality or state. When we look at these three points we find some hints as to how we can manage our loss and regain some control over our lives in the face of our present powerlessness.

Van Gennep's first observation about separating ourselves from our former state or status means that we must effectively sever our past ties or bonds with the deceased. This cannot be done quickly. It takes time and conscious effort on our part to do this. Considerable grief work has to be accomplished when we manage to get past this stage.

The second act of grief work consists in making changes which are necessary due to the loss. We need to act out in a healthy way. Public rituals, beginning with the time of the funeral, and subsequently as we talk about our loss to a compassionate friend offer us opportunities for the creative expression of our grief.

Our being able to participate in life again illustrates the third important task of grief work. Withdrawal from society indicates that the necessary adjustments have not been accomplished. During bereavement we need to be encouraged to participate in social events.

Our feelings of powerlessness and inability to manage our lives are normal responses to the loss of a loved one. Only when a person loses contact with reality and embraces grief in an unhealthy way such as by becoming very depressed can we speak of it as an illness. In sharing with others, we come to see and appreciate how we all have similar feelings about loss and its aftermath. The following exercises will help to put step one into better focus.

Focusing Exercises

1. Describe your feelings of powerlessness in the face of grief.

_____

_____

_____

2. Describe the effect grief has on your behavior.

_____

_____

_____

3. Can you recall early childhood memories of loss? Describe them and how you remember feeling at the time.

_____

_____

_____

4. List some ways that you can better manage your life.

_____

_____

_____

5. Are there any aspects of grief work which you are not addressing?

_____

_____

_____

_____

_____

The first step sets the tone for further steps. When we do well in identifying grief and its role, healing can begin. These six steps lead us on our journey through this loss. They will probably entail reliving and finishing some old business. That is only natural. It is when we are able to connect our past feelings to the present that we can then chart a healthy course to the future.

Journal Notes: (You may wish to acquire a separate notebook for your journal notes.)

_____

_____

_____

_____

_____

_____

_____

_____

_____

_____

_____

STEP TWO

Affirm that a Power greater than we can restore our balance.

These steps are a spiritual program. They require us to look at how our beliefs influence our lives. If we are used to living only in one dimension which preoccupies us with only the physical and material, then this step is a challenge. It requires some rethinking about reality as we live it.

Practicing this second step is in itself a process. In it we find a growing awareness of the need for a Power greater than ourselves to help us through our crisis and beyond.

Recently I overheard a sponsor and member of a step program as they were walking outside at the end of a meeting. When asked how things were going, the member replied, "I'm doing alright with my Higher Power." I was struck not only by the remark but by the way it was spoken — so spontaneously. It became clear to me that this individual had a genuine rapport with God as he conceived him. This indicated a growth and awareness which was "given to him" not by accident but rather by design in a step program. Living in one dimension means living without experiencing transcendence. We cannot believe in a Higher Power without looking at the expectations we have of ourselves and of others. Have we been created and empowered to go beyond ourselves, to transcend the very real limitations of our human nature? Is meditation a necessity for harmony, balance, and wholeness in our lives?

Achieving a balance within ourselves is an underlying goal behind our attempts to successfully live the steps. There is more to life than longevity. Life finds meaning when we achieve balance and harmony. Are we willing to live life as a whole person?

Letting Go

Finding a way to let go of our grief is necessary for progress in our recovery from any loss. We often hear the phrase, "I have to let go." But "let go" to where or better still to whom? "Let go and let God" is a phrase familiar to anyone knowledgeable about a successful step program. Accepting a Higher Power is a faith response to loss. Learning to trust again starts with a leap of faith. This leap is hardly a blind one. It is an informed and empowered leap fueled by a spiritual world view. Death has a way of awakening in us new perspectives on life.

This step may be approached in a variety of ways. The approach which treats the Higher Power as a philosophical/theological possibility, subject to proof will only end in failure. Arguments, rational possibilities, and other theories may be helpful but they are not what this step is all about. There has to occur a gradual awakening and acceptance of the transcendent, spiritual dimension to life.

The Russian novel, *The Brothers Karamazov*, speaks in a very down-to-earth way about the spiritual dimension of life. The questions posed in this 19th-century novel about the afterlife are universal and as valid today as they were back then. A woman is searching for the "answer" about whether there is life after death. She talks with the novel's wise and saintly monk, Father Zossima who gently responds to her questions. When we listen to his response we can apply the words to our own questions and fears as we struggle with belief and trust in a Higher Power.

> There's no proving it, though you can be convinced of it.... How? By the experience of active love. Strive to love your neighbor actively and indefatigably. In as far as you advance in love you will grow surer of the reality of God and of the immortality of your soul. If you attain to perfect self-forgetfulness in the love of your neighbor, then you will believe without doubt, and no doubt can possibly enter your soul. This has been tried. This is certain. (Fyodor Dostoyevsky, *The*

Brothers Karamazov, tr. from the Russian by Constance Garnett [NY: Modern Library, Random House], p. 55)

The monk's words capture the spirit of this step. Rather than stress some kind of a "self help" approach, this step offers so much more. The step allows us to place our position and person in creation into focus. Our reliance is not on some theory or even another human being. Rather we experience through our relationships the Ultimate Ground of our existence.

A step program with a strong spiritual foundation cannot be self-centered. If anything, it is eminently altruistic. We think of ourselves in terms of our relationships with our Higher Power and with others and seek to order our lives in the light of these relationships. In such a transcendent view, we can hardly think of the program as a mere expression of secular humanistic values. It is thoroughly theistic in its approach to life.

Practicing Trust

Relying on our Higher Power is a source of enormous consolation to us as we work through our grief. Through this Reality all else can be filtered. Comforting images of hope can resolve devastating feelings. Symptoms of bereavement such as emptiness, searching, yearning to be with the loved one, anger, abandonment, guilt, and others can be channeled through dialog with our Higher Power. Perhaps that is what the step participant's conversation with his sponsor which I overheard was really all about. There had been difficulties with his Higher Power in the past. Now, through dialog (meditating, praying) with God, the participant was not only coping with some very important issues in his life but was resolving them in a healthy and constructive way.

There can be difficulties in relating to God. It is not uncommon for the bereaved to blame God for what has happened. It really does not help anyone during a crisis to try to deal with who causes what to anyone. At that time we really are not able to conduct a rational conversation about the event.

Causes and Critical Events

In our Western society the Judeo-Christian tradition influences our view of God and causality. When the Jewish people encountered critical events they tended to ascribe everything directly to God. Secondary causes for such things as catastrophes never entered into their thinking. For example, if I were walking across the street and was suddenly hit and killed by a car, the way it might be reported in the Bible could read: "The hand of the Lord struck him down."

Even now, according to many belief systems, God is the direct and immediate cause of all that happens. However, as Roman Catholics we believe that God is not always the proximate cause for death. Nature, technology, human error, and accidents are but a few of the reasons why disasters occur that occasionally end in death. When we talk with children about death, it is always best to cite these natural causes. This allows the child to realistically assess what has happened and to keep a loving image of God.

All of these things have to be sorted out in the course of our grieving. Often clergy and counselors will remind their clients that God in Jesus wept, too, at the death of his friend, Lazarus. It is necessary during bereavement to recall this compassionate and loving image of God. It is all part of a needed spiritual reawakening which does occur as we reorganize our lives.

Indwelling Love

"God is love, and whoever abides in love abides in God and God in him" (1 Jn 4:8). This love which we experience from others and feel within our own hearts is an experience of the very presence of God, our Higher Power. While we grieve we need to go within ourselves and allow ourselves to be touched and consoled by the love which comes from others. The indwelling presence of God empowers us on our journey.

The traditional elements in this second step are meant to restore "sanity" to our lives. When we consider grief there is a need to use a better word than "sanity." "Balance" perhaps expresses the concept more adequately because it implies the need to be in harmony. It also helps not to confuse what is normal and natural in the grieving process with an illness. Anyone who has experienced a death or other critical event in life is thrown off balance. We need reassurance that we are not mentally ill. Everything in our lives is chaotic for awhile and self-doubt does creep into our consciousness. We need others to be aware that we are not ourselves and will not be for awhile. At this critical time we need to know that the feelings we are experiencing are a necessary part of our eventual healing.

While we journey through this step we need to be hopeful. Our relationship with God and others can help by providing us with healing images. We have to express our true feelings at this time and let our complaints be known. We should not hesitate to cry out to God and others. This is how we release the tension we feel and ritualize our loss so that our lives can go through the needed transformation.

Focusing With Step Two

1. How can I come to experience the presence of a Higher Power in my life?

_____

_____

_____

_____

2. Are there obstacles in my relationship with God?

_____

_____

_____

_____

_____

3. What is needed to restore balance to my life?

_____

_____

_____

_____

_____

4. What hope do I have for my future here on earth as I consider it in the light of my belief in the afterlife?

_____

_____

_____

_____

_____

5. What results do I experience in calling upon my Higher Power?

_____

_____

_____

_____

_____

_____

_____

STEP THREE

Freely turn ourselves toward God and let God take charge of our lives and healing.

Anyone who has done crisis work with the bereaved knows what not to do; others frequently make some serious mistakes. When a death occurs it is an assault to a person's psyche. The individual is in shock and needs time to sort out exactly what you are saying. A real mistake is made when platitudes are used at this time. They hinder acceptance of the event and do future harm to the person's grieving process.

One of the most common errors is to say: "It's God's will." This is often too much for the grief stricken person to hear. At this point in time they are just not ready. Another point to consider is that they may be very angry with God. As we noted earlier, many attribute direct causality to God when a death occurs.

Some crisis interventionists tell us that if such a remark as "It's God's will" is made you have a very good chance of making an atheist out of someone. In other words the opposite to the intended result occurs.

The phrasing of this step has been changed. Instead of a past tense of the verb the active voice is used. To turn ourselves toward God illustrates that we have to freely make an effort to accept and conform our will to the source of our life. Acceptance does not come easily for any of us.

This step is very likely to be camouflaged by the bereaved. It is not acceptable to be angry with God. People get upset when you tell them that. They just do not know how to respond. The bereaved feel that rather than suffer more alienation it is better to placate and deny their true feelings for the sake of others.

Conforming To God's Will

There can be no conformity to God's will or acceptance without expressing our real feelings. People sometimes need permission to say how they really feel. They often need to cry out as they tell their story. This ought to be encouraged as part of this step.

Conformity to God's will does not mean some kind of blind obedience or acceptance. It means bringing our real self to dialog with God. It means owning our feelings and not denying them.

Thomas Merton's Meditation

"My Lord God, I have no idea where I am going. I do not see the road ahead of me. I cannot know for certain where it will end. Nor do I really know myself, and the fact that I think I am following your will does not mean that I am actually doing so. But I believe that the desire to please you does in fact please you. And I hope I have that desire in all that I am doing. I hope that I will never do anything apart from that desire. And I know that if I do this you will lead me by the right road though I may know nothing about it. Therefore will I trust you always though I may seem to be lost and in the shadow of death. I will not fear, for you are ever with me, and you will never leave me to face my perils alone."

Conforming our will to that of God must be done according to the state of our psyche. We hear in Thomas Merton's prayer an accurate appraisal of how we really feel. The mystical monk knows how difficult it is to want to please God. There is no denial of our confusion at times. This is especially pertinent when applied to the way we think and feel during bereavement. Our acceptance of God's will comes in spite of our confusion and hurt. His prayer is a healing prayer which does not permit us to take refuge in denial. Rather, it honestly puts into focus how chaotic our lives are when there is a loss and expresses our desire to move on from there.

When we live this third step we are "letting go" in a more mystical manner. It is unfortunate that clinicians have taken over the phrase "letting go," reducing it to something thought to be observable only by psychological scrutiny. The phrase really can mean letting go into the hands of God. This demonstrates how important beliefs become when we examine phrases. The spiritual resolution of grief has everything to offer us.

Focusing Suggestions For Step Three

1. Find some time to read over Thomas Merton's meditation.
2. Become more familiar with your belief about the Kingdom of God.
3. Pray the Our Father very slowly emphasizing acceptance of God's will.
4. For a complete meditation on the Our Father you may want to refer to the *Catechism of the Catholic Church*.
5. List in your journal what areas of your life still need to be conformed to God's will.

STEP FOUR

Examine our relationships and attachments to better understand ourselves and what is happening.

The story is told of the father who wanted to keep his young son busy. He decided to cut up the cover of a magazine with a beautifully colored picture of the world on one side. This global picture would serve as a puzzle and occupy the child while the parent took care of other things. No sooner had the father started on his own project than he heard the child tell him that he had finished the puzzle.

The father was amazed when he saw the completed work in front of him. The child was asked how he did this so quickly. His reply was simply, "It was easy." His son told him that on the other side of the puzzle was the picture of a man and woman.

This story says something important about life. If we put together the picture of our relationships with others then our world will come together. All of our attachments color our way of relating to one another. If these attachments are disordered, our lives will not make much sense. This tells us that our world view may be lacking something. Without a comprehensive overview of life our lives will be chaotic.

It is necessary to constantly assess our relationships. How do we see our encounters with others? If we are possessive or controlling then our world view will be one of continual frustration.

Grief Work

Grief work entails performing certain tasks as we try to put together the areas of our lives which have become for us a very real puzzle. There are many pieces which have to be sorted out. We have to accept that our world and our relationships have gotten jumbled and have to be put together again, this time in a new way. It is important that we know ourselves if this is to be accomplished successfully.

Self-assessment can be very painful. Very often we cannot do this as we just do not possess the ability to be objective. We need to ask the right questions about ourselves if we are to accurately assess our ability to grieve in ways which will bring about healing. Mistaken remedies for grief only cause our lives more pain. Denial through drugs and other diversions only postpone healing. This is unfortunately the route taken by many in our society.

Courage To Grieve

It takes courage to grieve in authentic ways. Soul searching is necessary to know ourselves and what may be causing some complications in our grief. We can be our own worst enemy when we do not face our losses. Denial only complicates our grief and prolongs unnecessary suffering.

All of us can delude ourselves into thinking that we are stronger than we really are. We can easily give ourselves credit for being more self-possessed and equipped to handle difficulties than is true. We need to be more reality based in making our assessments of ourselves. When we get a truer picture of ourselves, then we can seek help in those areas of weakness. At the same time our strengths will be seen as a resource.

History of Loss

Before we look at a grief inventory it is a good idea to develop a history of our losses. This is similar to mapping out significant events or moments in our lives. If we recall our initial losses and our reactions and responses to them then we can appreciate how we have either succeeded or failed in the past.

Mapping significant losses gives a realistic interpretation to our journey. We do not want to fall into the trap of idealizing our lives. There could have been, and most probably were, significant losses in our childhood. Only much later do we recall them and realize what an impact they had on our lives.

Our initial loss may have been that of a pet. Or it may have been the loss of a friend who had to move to another location. Being young we may not have grieved or known how to grieve in a conscious way. Memories of a classmate who died may at the time have seemed more of a point of wonder than loss. Only later did we come to realize that our friend was not going to come to school anymore.

Childhood is where we must begin our mapping of loss. As we move into adolescence we experience the loss of childhood. This is oftentimes a loss overlooked and not properly grieved.

There are multiple primary losses which we can recall. It is also very important to connect these primary losses with our secondary ones. Secondary losses are consequences to a loss. They are considered secondary not because they are unimportant. That is by far not the case. They are secondary because they follow upon a primary loss.

The loss of a dream or a hope for the future can be devastating. This is apparent, for example, in the case of a miscarriage. Everything was set up in the room waiting for the baby who did not come home. There occurs a shattering which requires considerable time for regaining a sense of equilibrium in life again for the couple struggling with such a loss.

It can be very helpful to chart our losses, not out of a sense of being morbid but as a healthy exercise which gives us insights into how we deal with separation and loss in our lives. Our goal is to be more knowledgeable about how to manage our losses. If we fail to do this then we risk having our losses manage us!

Our chart can be made in a simple way by years of loss. For example the graph may start in 1953 with the death of a pet. Or, it could include the loss of a friend for any number of reasons. The death of a grandparent, aunt, or uncle may follow. The early experiences of death color our childhood.

The chart or graph is a visual aid to discussing loss with a compassionate listener. It helps to put into perspective how our journey has been to date.

Focusing Suggestions For Step Four

Developing a Grief Inventory

A grief inventory can focus on our attitudes on loss. The inventory can help again with our discussions with compassionate listeners. It can identify for us our emotions and, through reflection, help us to understand ourselves and the grieving process in a more succinct way.

The inventory can begin with questions similar to our charting of loss. The questions will continue to include some important emotional aspects to loss. We may want to choose a trusted friend or compassionate listener to help us with this self assessment. An inventory of this type is meant to be descriptive. The data is by far more qualitative than quantitative. It is meant not so much to be a measurable instrument as a healing tool for the bereaved.

Sample Inventory Questions

1. Recall your earliest experience of loss.

_____

_____

_____

2. Briefly describe the incident as you believe you experienced it at that time.

_____

_____

_____

3. What emotion would you say was most prevalent?

_____

_____

_____

_____

4. How do you feel you worked through your feelings about this loss?

_____

_____

_____

_____

_____

5. Do you feel that there is still unfinished grief stemming from this loss?

_____

_____

_____

_____

6. Was there anyone who was of considerable help? If so who? And how?

_____

_____

_____

_____

_____

7. Did your religious faith play a role in dealing with the loss?

_____

_____

_____

_____

_____

_____

8. Do you remember whether prayer or eternal life were mentioned?

_____

_____

_____

_____

_____

_____

The preceding questions are not easy to answer. We can appreciate the need to have courage in confronting loss. We also must be aware of the need to have significant others in our lives to assist us. In step programs a sponsor is a significant person. The compassionate listener has to assume many of the characteristics of trust similar to a sponsor.

STEP FIVE

Learn to love and trust again. Form a new spiritual relationship with the loved one who has died.

The Christian response to death is always that life is not ended, merely changed. These words from the Preface of the Funeral Mass illustrate the task of redefining our relationship with the person who has died.

As Catholics, we hold to belief in the Communion of Saints. It is the constant prayer of the Church on earth that all will enter that communion with God in the Kingdom of Heaven. Through our beliefs we are able to express in signs and symbols a new relationship with those who have gone before us.

Catholic tradition is rich in resources for this all important task of grief work. Everything from lighting a votive candle to having a Memorial Mass offered for the deceased is part and parcel of Catholicism. Those who have died are always remembered in the context of faith.

The Eucharistic Celebration is the central act of worship. During every Mass there is a remembrance of the dead. Every Mass is offered for everyone, but there are special remembrances of the dead which bring peace and consolation to the bereaved.

Ritual Actions

Ritual actions connect us with the power of God. Our very being is energized or graced by connecting with what the ritual symbolizes. We see this in everyday life. The gesture of shaking hands with someone is a public ritual which illustrates connecting with another human being. The ritual is supposed to symbolize a binding and, as we release, a letting go. Our intention in performing this action publicly is all important. If it is only a perfunctory social act then the real meaning is lost.

Religious rituals have a way of binding together our beliefs about reality as we perceive it. Through rituals we are able to express ourselves as spiritual beings. Rituals are instruments which help us to remember.

Liturgy

Through liturgy we are able to celebrate communal rituals. Our rituals commemorate those who now worship with us in spirit and truth. They also, through our faith, help us to pray for those who are awaiting entrance to the Kingdom of God.

Our rituals remind us to pray for those who have died. They are not nor do they allow what is known as "idealizing." We are well too aware of our need for prayers and that we are sinners. Idealizing occurs when we deny the shadow side of human personalities.

Through signs and symbols we express our loss. Funeral liturgies are the initial rituals in our public expression of grief which we call mourning. To convert our mourning into grace we need to come together and express our loss.

Redefining Our Relationship

Very often we hear that grief is incomplete until it finds expression. How many people do you know who complain: "I really never got the chance to say good-bye." Rituals remind us that life is eternal and so we are still able to relate to those whom we love even after they are gone.

There may be other emotions which must be properly channeled. We may have guilt that needs to be resolved. Reconciliation is possible through asking and praying for forgiveness. Anger often surfaces at the time of a death. "How could he leave me?" We need to realize that normal reactions to loss need to be placed into a context which can then be dealt with in a healthy way.

The praying of the Psalms has been a way of ritualizing a loss from time immemorial. In praying the Psalms we give vent to those emotions which are so often denied. We cry out to God, we wonder aloud about life's meaning, and we learn to trust again.

A wonderful ritual is to compose your own Psalm. We have noted the importance of the Psalms in Part II, the Personal Prayer Guide. Along with the Psalms we highly recommend the Way of the Cross and the recitation of the Sorrowful Mysteries of the Rosary. Once again we look at our suffering and unite ourselves with Jesus in his agony.

Creative ways to redefine our relationships are necessary for all of us as we grieve. The many rituals we have that assist us in doing this help us to grieve in healing ways.

Focusing Suggestions For Step Five

1. In this step find a trusted friend to help you talk about what needs to be redefined in your grief.
2. Choose a ritual which you feel will help you remember in the context of faith. This could be a memorial Mass, Way of the Cross, composing a Psalm, recitation of the Rosary or other personal family rituals.
3. Family photographs and videos can trigger ways to remember loved ones.
4. Do not be afraid to cry.
5. You can ritualize certain tasks of grief. This is especially evident in putting possessions of the deceased away or in giving away possessions to family, friends, and charities.

STEP SIX

Having experienced healing and having our loved ones restored to us in the ways of the Spirit, bring that message of life beyond death to others who are suffering.

There is no time limit for grief. There are, in accordance with this step, moments of transformation and change. While we are grieving we can expect to see life in a different way. When we are able to sort things out and find some meaning behind our loss, we will find that our lives are noticeably different. In fact they will never be the same again.

The Psalmist reflects on this kind of change during times of loss and new awakenings in the words: "You have turned my mourning into dancing." Grief is converted into grace. We begin to see that we have a new relationship with the deceased. This may have been accomplished in a variety of ways.

The bereaved person doing this step must be aware of those things that have contributed to his or her being able to live in a balanced kind of way once again. What contributed to sorting out the chaos of their lives and how did they receive that awakening?

Once learned, how to go through grief is often best articulated by the bereaved themselves. Encouraging others who are grieving to go in the direction of the pain rather than to avoid it can be of very real help to them. Inviting them to join a support group and make a commitment to stay with the group is another important aid. Having them seek out a compassionate listener is also a very significant move in the right direction.

This step also helps us as we help others to realize some important aspects of self-esteem. We see ourselves in a different light as we relate to others who are grieving. Our inner resources and consequent ability to cope now become very clear to us. We need to appreciate this as we reach out in an unselfish way to others.

Becoming involved in helping others through grief ministry is not something we are always ready to do. Sometimes advice is given to wait at least a year before deciding to embark on this ministry. It would seem better to state that you ought to wait until you feel you are ready. This may take more than a year. To become involved too quickly could be a mistake. We unwittingly could be avoiding our own feelings by being with others.

There are many ways in the parish that we can share our experience of loss. This can be done through offering to assist or participate in pastoral programs which contribute to our spiritual growth. This step ought be the logical outcome of our receiving healing and consolation from others. It is very much in keeping with a selfless approach to our faith.

Focusing Suggestions for Step Six

1. As you journey through grief note in your journal what is awakening in you about your life.
2. Be aware that you must be cautious about when it is time to share your new approaches with others.
3. Seek guidance from others about the best way to continue growing since your loss.
4. Participate in spiritual enrichment groups or parish programs which will help with your spiritual growth.

PART II

Personal Prayer Guide

Prayers During Bereavement

We need to develop a spirituality for separation and loss. The only way to really accomplish such a difficult task is to do it. Prayer leads us to a peace beyond our understanding. Praying during bereavement is necessary for both remembering and letting go. They help our loved one's spirit in their journey to the Kingdom as they help ourselves. We too must continue our journey and we cannot do it without spiritual strength. Our spirits are weak and we often feel like retreating. We need to express our innermost thoughts and feelings. Bereavement and the accompanying chaos can be converted into a time of creativity and hope.

During bereavement we redefine our relationship with our deceased loved one. At the same time we often redefine our relationship with God. New images and realities are brought to our communication with God.

This section concerns itself with prayers. Prayers are offered at various times during our experience of loss. The prayers offered here are samples which may be used individually or with groups. These prayers mirror what the bereaved may be experiencing during the phases of grief.

Each prayer is not meant to be read and treated as some kind of an exercise. Rather they are gateways through which we journey. Through them we unlock the underlying feelings and the reality of God's grace. The prayers are our healing resource in faith.

When we pray them for the first time we may well be experiencing our own Good Friday. Taking this journey will bring us to Easter. In the Easter mysteries we find strength and are uplifted. Our transition will bring us out of darkness into light, from chaos to creation, and convert our grief into grace. We pray that as we meditate on these mysteries we truly imitate what they contain and initiate the experience of God's healing.

As we experience symptoms of grief — the confusion, sleeplessness, weighted sorrow and sighing — we stay with God and present our feelings for healing. The following prayer experiences are divided into three parts. (1) The introduction of themes to think about before reading the prayer or Psalm. (2) The Psalm itself or prayer. (3) Meditation on the particular prayer or Psalm when we work toward applying the Psalm to our own lives.

For support groups I would recommend that the leader paraphrase the meditation and pass out copies of the prayer. The group could then proceed with the meditation having been allowed suitable time for the participants to familiarize themselves with the prayer. The preceding suggestion is for a group. Other suitable adaptations may be made for individuals who want to use these for grief work.

Our prayers may introduce a parish support group, a special liturgy, or may be offered when we are alone at home. The prayer will help us to identify and accept our feelings and at the same time place our loss into the context of faith. We will rely on certain Psalms and some traditional Catholic prayers which have helped many Christians in the past. When we experience these prayers in the context of grief, healing is provided for our brokenness.

PRAYER EXPERIENCE ONE:
Introduction

When Loss Happens

The death of a loved one is a shock. We cry out in disbelief about the fact that someone we cared about has died. We need to express this fact. Our identifying with certain Psalms helps us to realize what has really happened. We can praise God by way of lamenting. During this initial phase of shock and numbness we have to own our emotions. We realize that we may have feelings of abandonment, guilt, emptiness, anger, and yearning to be with our loved one. These are threads we all share. These threads can be gossamer thin or thick cables that separate and even isolate us from others. Prayer helps us to express our grief with its gamut of emotions and at the same time places our loss into a wider context of meaning.

Prayer

Psalm 130

Out of the depths I cry to you, O Lord;
>   Lord hear my voice!
Let your ears be attentive
>   to my voice in supplication:
If you, O Lord, mark iniquities
>   Lord who can stand?
But with you is forgiveness,
>   that you may be revered.
I trust in the Lord;
>   my soul trusts in his word.
My soul waits for the Lord
>   more than sentinels wait for the dawn.

More than sentinels wait for the dawn,
    let Israel wait for the Lord.
For with the Lord is kindness
    and with him plenteous redemption;
And he will redeem Israel
    from all their iniquities.

Prayer Meditation

Allow yourself to find a quiet place. Read over the Psalm and then try to picture in your mind the mood and the setting. Closing your eyes acknowledge the depths you are experiencing. Do you feel alone in a crowd? Are you sitting in darkness with the weight of grief pressing down upon you? Do you feel adrift at sea with cruel waves of grief washing over you? In these depths can you also experience the whisper of Christ's presence, the breeze of his love, the constant beam of his light in the darkness? Can you see the Lord watching over you and sharing your grief? Do not hesitate to express yourself to him, crying out when the pain and reality seem too much to bear. He is there with the Psalmist as you acknowledge his continual presence. Trust in the Lord and wait for the Lord's help. Seek deliverance from the shock and assault of death.

Grief Notes: In this section you can record some of your initial reactions to loss.

_____

_____

_____

_____

_____

_____

_____

PRAYER EXPERIENCE TWO:
Guidance Through Grief

Introduction

No one of us is able to live without others. We are not self-sufficient. We need to connect with others if we are to have a purposeful life.

As we grieve there is the temptation to think that we can resolve matters by ourselves. We retreat from interacting with others as we get drawn into the chaos in our lives. If ever there is a need to be with others it is while we are grieving.

We need others to hear our story. Friends, willing to listen, help us to sort out our feelings. They act as guides through the emptiness and darkness. They are signposts to tell us how we are doing.

Going through the darkness is only possible because we are given the grace and the ability to do so. When Jesus prayed the Psalms he did this in communion with God the Father. Jesus in his oneness with the Father experienced the fullness of the Father's love. He has shown us how to share in the Father's love by calling on the Father for his assistance.

Prayer

Psalm 23
The Lord Is My Shepherd

The Lord is my shepherd,
    I shall not want.
In verdant pastures
    he gives me repose;
Beside restful waters he leads me;
    he refreshes my soul.

He guides me in right paths
for his name's sake.
Even though I walk in the dark valley
I fear no evil;
for you are at my side
With your rod and your staff
that give me courage.
You spread the table before me
in the sight of my foes;
You anoint my head with oil;
my cup overflows.
Only goodness and kindness follow me
all the days of my life;
And I shall dwell in the house of the Lord
for years to come.

Prayer Meditation

This Psalm is rich in imagery. It draws us in and solidifies our relationship with God as our Shepherd. Its exquisite imagery of ourselves as sheep being led through the dark valley by the strong arm of our Lord is easy to picture. Even the setting gives form to our grief.

We cannot traverse the dark valley of death without help. Letting go really means experiencing communion. Letting go means dying to our selves and rising to others. The Transcendent One is the Lord who is our guide. God is our loving Other who cares for us and leads us. Reflect on how God provides guidance through others. Picture someone who truly cares and wants to help us through the pain we are experiencing to the Ultimate Peace which awaits us.

You may wish to play softly some comforting instrumental music as you meditate on Psalm 23. Allow yourself to become more in harmony with life. You are still seeking a sense of balance. It is the Spirit who breathes life and gives form to our existence.

Grief Notes: Use this space to take an inventory of your life. List people who have been loving and caring.

_____

_____

_____

_____

_____

_____

_____

_____

_____

_____

_____

_____

_____

_____

_____

_____

_____

_____

_____

_____

_____

_____

PRAYER EXPERIENCE THREE:
"Feelings of Abandonment"

Introduction

We need to connect our emotions with our religious faith. Connecting means admitting, not denying, our feelings. Through the Psalms we express our feelings of anger, emptiness, and abandonment, and cry out as the Psalmist did attempting to sort out what was really happening.

At this time we may not be able to see ourselves trusting again. As we experience the Psalms we realize that more changes are going to occur in our grief. When we identify with the Psalmist we recognize ourselves in the struggle for meaning and hope in life.

The Psalms give form or structure to our lives. We may be disoriented or numb and need to express ourselves. In the Psalms poetic expression is allowed. Permission to be ourselves and converse with God in a passionate way is given to us.

Very often when we lose a loved one in death we feel desperately alone. Our minds become confused by the loss. We think we have been completely abandoned and wonder what is happening to us. Consolation and new ways of realizing our connectedness to the entire human condition are affirmed in the Psalms. The following Psalm is one we are all familiar with as Christians. Jesus prayed this Psalm on the cross.

Prayer

Psalm 22:1-6

My God, my God, why have you forsaken me,
    far from my prayer, from the words of my cry?
O my God, I cry out by day, and you answer not;
    by night, and there is no relief for me.
Yet you are enthroned in the holy place,

O glory of Israel!
In you our fathers trusted;
   they trusted, and you delivered them.
To you they cried, and they escaped;
   in you they trusted, and they were not put to shame.

Prayer Meditation

Picture yourself telling the Psalm writer about your loss. You may even want to picture yourself composing a Psalm as was done at the Temple. You are crying out by day and by night. The presence of loss is weighing you down. You need relief as did the one seeking help in this Psalm. Is there any relief in sight? What can be done? How can I seek the Lord?

Allow yourself to cry out to the Lord. Call upon the name of the Lord. God does not turn away his face from us.

As we feel the steadfast trust that gave our forefathers courage amidst their trials and tribulations we can sense a shift from despair to trust. When you feel a change of mood continue reading this Psalm (22:23-27). Our hearts can be uplifted once again as we worship in the assembly.

Grief Notes:

_____

_____

_____

_____

_____

_____

_____

_____

PRAYER EXPERIENCE FOUR:
"When Grief Is Longing and Yearning"

Introduction

Crisis professionals tell us that when someone dies they are more present to us than perhaps at any other time. Their lives and our relationship to them become fine tuned. They take on a brightness in the gray tones of our memories. Mannerisms, events, and even what we thought were long forgotten are recalled. Memories of our loved one flood into our consciousness. This is how we realize that someone so very close to us has died.

The initial grief phase has been described as shock. We are numb and need to process what has happened. While we recall that our loved one has died, we wish that we could see them again. After the funeral this yearning and wanting to see the deceased for many becomes even more pronounced. Returning to an empty house and being reminded by so many things makes us wish we were with our loved one once again.

Wanting to see or be with our loved one is an appropriate reaction to the loss. Sometimes this yearning is not adequately expressed. It is difficult to say how we feel. The Psalmist helps us to express this deep and intense feeling.

Prayer

Psalm 42:1-6

As the deer longs for the running streams,
    so my soul longs for you, O God.
Athirst is my soul for God, the living God.
    When shall I go and behold the face of God?
My tears are my food day and night,
    as they say to me day after day,

"Where is your God?"
Those times I recall,
    now that I pour out my soul within me,
When I went with the throng
    and led them in procession to the house of God,
Amid loud cries of joy and thanksgiving,
    with the multitude keeping festival.
Why are you downcast, O my soul?
    Why do you sigh within me?
Hope in God! For I shall again be thanking him,
    in the presence of my savior and my God.

Prayer Meditation

We must go in the direction of pain while we grieve. The vivid imagery of Psalm 42 draws out the grief we are experiencing. Rather than the waves of sorrow, now we long for words and gestures of peace, but they go unspoken or unacknowledged. We search for our lost time. When we avoid or deny our memories and thoughts we only make matters worse. It is painful yet necessary to recall what our loved one was like. You can imagine their face and those expressions which were uniquely theirs.

The poet describes our feelings. "O for the touch of a vanished hand and the sound of a voice that is gone."[1] Even though we want our loved one to be with us we realize now that everything has changed.

Our comfort and consolation is in the Lord who made our loved one as he made the heavens and the earth. We look forward to our Heavenly reunion. It is that sure hope which gives our yearning and longing purpose.

---

[1] Alfred Lord Tennyson, "Break, Break, Break."

Grief Notes:

_____

_____

_____

_____

_____

_____

_____

_____

_____

_____

_____

_____

_____

_____

_____

_____

_____

_____

_____

_____

_____

_____

_____

PRAYER EXPERIENCE FIVE:
"When we need relief from grief"

Introduction

When we grieve it seems that it will never end. We question ourselves and life itself as to the duration. We need to realize that there is no time limit for loss. Grief is unlike anything else. It surfaces when we least expect it. Our grief changes as our lives proceed. Yet we continue to cry out to God.

We need to go through a transformation. Such a change is not possible by ourselves alone. We need to converse with God regarding our sorrow. We need assistance.

Very often we feel terribly disoriented. We question our psychological health. Once again we have to appreciate that we are not ill. Grief is part of life and must be seen in that context. Unfortunately we live in a society that thinks pain is synonymous with illness.

Our souls must endure the many colors of life. We need to pay attention to these colors to be truly alive. The following Psalm prayer relates to our need to be heard not only by God. We need to hear ourselves becoming more aware of our grief and its impact on us. We ask for assistance amidst a death-denying culture. Our foe is our throw-away culture which discards the young and the old. It tells us that grief is over when the funeral ends. It falsely instructs us to get on with everything and forget the past. Amidst the denial God hears and heals.

Prayer

Psalm 13

How long, O Lord? Will you utterly forget me?
How long will you hide your face from me?

How long shall I harbor sorrow in my soul,
    this grief in my heart day after day?
How long will my enemy triumph over me?
    Look, answer me, O Lord my God!
Give light to my eyes that I may not sleep in death
    lest my enemy say, "I have overcome him"
Lest my foes rejoice at my downfall
    though I trusted your kindness.
Let my heart rejoice in your salvation;
    let me sing of the Lord,
        "He has been good to me."

Prayer Meditation

Loving God, help me to go through this time of loss. Allow me to realize that my suffering will not go on forever. With you is redemption. Your healing presence opens my eyes. I am beginning to realize that my suffering will be converted to joy. You will help me to trust and love again. My heart rejoices in your salvation. You will keep my love alive amidst denials. I will experience communion with God and with my loved one.

Grief Notes: Describe how heavy your heart has been during this time of separation and loss.

_____

_____

_____

_____

_____

_____

PRAYER EXPERIENCE SIX:
Acceptance

Introduction

It takes considerable time to accept that our loss has really occurred. We have already been told that we must "let go." Sometimes this advice irritates us. We really do not want to forget. There is so much that we want to embrace.

Grief means remembering and also moving on and creating new memories. Our letting go is not into the void. Our letting go is accepting that our loved one is hopefully going forth to the Kingdom. Our prayers are for them to complete the journey in the Reign of God.

We must accept our separation and loss in the context of faith. Our consolation as Christians goes far beyond "coping." We live and breathe and have our being with the power of the Kingdom breaking into our lives as we establish a new mode of communion with our loved one.

Prayer

Let us pray....

We seem to give _____ back to you, Lord, who gave him/her to us. Yet as you did not lose him/her in giving so we do not lose him/her by his/her return.

Not as the world gives do you give. What you give you do not take away, for if we are your children, what is yours is ours also. For us, life is eternal and love is immortal.

Death is only the horizon and the horizon is nothing but the limit of our sight.

Help us, Lord Jesus, that we may see further. Cleanse our eyes that we may see more clearly; draw us closer to you so that we know ourselves to be nearer to _____ who is now with you.

While you prepare a place for us, prepare us also for that happy place that where you are we may be also forever. (Anonymous)

Prayer Meditation

This prayer may be recited often during our grief. It is especially helpful during the early phases of loss. During the first few months we need to accept that our loved one has died. Meditating on the mystery of life as a gift given back to God is enlightening and healing.

Meditation is a contemplative action which gives new shape to our loss. St. Augustine tells us that: "What the parched soul longs for may be found in a quiet place."

Find a quiet place to read over this prayer of acceptance. Spend some time contemplating the mystery. A few moments a day will help your mood as you ponder the mystery.

BIBLIOGRAPHICAL REFERENCES & PASTORAL TOPICS

Suffering & Grief

Curley, Terence P. "Light in Darkness," *Praying Magazine* (Nov.-Dec.) No. 57, 1993.

Dean, James. "Grief and Attachment," *Journal of Religion and Health*, Vol. 27, No. 2 (157-165) Summer, 1988.

Del Zoppo, Patrick M. *Mourning: The Journey from Grief to Healing.* New York: Alba House, 1995.

Kushner, Harold. *When Bad Things Happen To Good People.* New York: Avon Books, 1981.

_____. *When All You've Ever Wanted Isn't Enough.* New York: Pocket Books, 1986.

Kutscher, Austin H. *A Bibliography of Books on Death, Bereavement, and Grief: 1935-1968.* New York: Health Sciences Publications, 1969.

Lewis, C.S. *A Grief Observed.* New York: Bantam Books, 1961.

Lindemann, Erich. "Symptomatology and Management of Acute Grief," *American Journal of Psychiatry* 101, (141-148), 1944.

Rando, Therese A. *Grief, Dying, And Death: Clinical Interventions For Caregivers.* Illinois: Research Press Co., 1984.

Vernick, Joel J. *Selected Bibliography on Death and Dying.* Maryland: U.S. National Institute of Health, 1969.

Viorst, Judith. *Necessary Losses.* New York: Ballantine Books, 1986.

Wise, Barbara. *Grief.* New York: Alba House, 1994.

Sudden Infant Death Syndrome (SIDS)

Donnelly, K.F. *Recovering From the Loss of a Child.* New York: Macmillan, 1982.

Littlefield, C.H. "When A Child Dies: The Sociobiology of Bereave-ment," *Journal of Personality and Social Psychology*, 51 (4), 797-802.

Wright, A.L. "Models of Mystery: Physician and Patient Perceptions of Sudden Infant Death Syndrome." *Social Science Medicine*, 26 (6), 587-595.

Loss & Children

Bowlby, John. *Attachment and Loss*. Vol. III. New York: Basic Books. 1980.

Curley, Terence P. "The Child's Experience of Loss," *The Priest*, Vol. 48, No. 5. May, 1992, p. 36.

_____. "The Grieving Child and Religious Formation," *Pastoral Life*, Vol. 45, No. 1. January, 1996.

Grollman, Earl A. *Explaining Death To Children*. Boston: Beacon Press, 1968.

Jewett, Claudia. *Helping Children Cope with Separation and Loss*. Harvard, MA: Harvard Press, 1982.

Kubler-Ross, Elisabeth. *On Children and Death*. New York: Macmillan, 1983.

Vogel, Linda. *Helping A Child Understand Death*. Philadelphia: Fortress Press, 1975.

Acquired Immunodeficiency Syndrome (AIDS)

Bohne, J. "AIDS: Ministry issues for Chaplains," *Pastoral Psychology*, 1986, 34 (3), 173-192.

Ellens, J.H. "AIDS: The Pastor and Patient-Parishioner," *Journal of Psychology and Christianity*, 1987, 6 (3), 1924.

Menz, R.L. "Aiding Those With AIDS: A Mission For The Church," *Journal of Psychology and Christianity*, 1987, 6 (3), 518.

Smith, Walter J., S.J. *AIDS: Living & Dying with Hope*. New York: Paulist Press, 1988.

The Elderly & Loss

Sullender, R. Scott. *Grief and Growth: Pastoral Resources for Emotional and Spiritual Growth.* New York: Paulist Press, 1985.
_____ *Losses In Later Life.* New York: Paulist Press, 1989.

Miscarriage

Baily, R. *For Everything A Season.* Hawthorne Books, 1975.
Curley, Terence P. "When a Child Dies." *Celebration*, Vol. 22, No. 11 (November 1993), 438-440.
Friedman, R. and Gradstein, B. *Surviving Pregnancy Loss.* Boston: Little Brown & Co., 1982.
Pizer, H. Palenski, O'Brien, C. *Coping with a Miscarriage.* New York: The Deal Press, 1980.

Widows

Anders, Sarah F. *Woman Alone, Confident and Creative.* Nashville: Broadman Press, 1976.
Caine, Lynn. *Widow.* Toronto: Bantam Books, 1974.
Curry, Cathleen L. *When Your Spouse Dies.* Notre Dame, IN.: Ave Maria Press, 1990.
Roberts-Drucker, Margaret A. *Companion to My Tears.* New York: Alba House, 1994.
Start, Clarissa. *When You're a Widow.* St. Louis: Concordia Publishing, 1968.

Death From Suicide

Alvarez, Alfred. *The Savage God: A Study of Suicide.* New York: Random House, 1972.

Douglas, Jack D. *The Social Meaning of Suicide.* Princeton, N.J.:
    Princeton University Press, 1967.
Grollman, Earl A. *Suicide: Prevention, Intervention, Postvention.*
    Boston: Beacon Press, 1971.
Lum, Doman. *Responding to Suicidal Crisis: For Church and Commu-
    nity.* Grand Rapids: Eerdmans, 1974.

Ministry and Loss

Brueggeman, Walter. "From Hurt To Joy, From Death to Life,"
    Interpretation, XXXVIII, No. 1 (320) January, 1974.
Clinebell, Howard J. *Basic Types of Pastoral Care and Counseling:
    Resources for the Ministry of Healing & Growth.* Nashville:
    Abingdon Press, 1984.
Curley, Terence P. *The Ministry of Consolation: A Parish Guide for
    Comforting the Bereaved.* New York: Alba House, 1993.
_____ *Healing the Broken-Hearted: Comforting the Grief-Stricken.*
    New York: Alba House, 1995.
_____ *Relating the Roman Catholic Order of Christian Funerals
    (1989) to the Needs of the Bereaved in a Parish.* Boston,
    MA: Boston University Library, 1990.
_____ . "The Order of Christian Funerals: A Better Connection
    for Pastoral Care," *The Priest*, Vol. 47, No. 4 (43) April,
    1991.
_____ "Psalms for Separation and Loss," *The Priest*. Vol. 47, No.
    11 (41) November, 1991.
_____ . "Organizing a Parish Bereavement Committee," *The
    Priest*, Vol. 48, No. 10 (54) October, 1992.
_____ . "Establishing a Caring Group to Support the Bereaved,"
    Pastoral Life, Vol. 40, No. 10 (17) November, 1991.
_____ . "Disasters and the Pastoral Response," *The Priest*, Vol.
    52, No. 2. February, 1996.
Pinkava, Mary Jane. "Consoling Presence, Heart of Bereavement
    Ministry," *Modern Liturgy*, Vol. 19, No. 7 (14) 1992.
Spakes, Robert, and Richard Rutherford. "The Order of Christian

Funerals: A Study in Bereavement and Lament," *Worship*, 60, No. 6 (1986) (499).

Sullender, R. Scott. *Grief and Growth: Pastoral Resources for Emotional and Spiritual Growth*. New York: Paulist Press, 1985.

Switzer, David. *The Minister as Crisis Counselor*. Nashville: Abingdon Press, 1974.

Williams, Donna Reilly. "Let's Allow Mourners A Time to Heal," *Modern Liturgy*, Vol. 19, No. 7 (20) 1992.

Liturgy And Loss

Boadt, Lawrence, Mary Dombeck, and H. Richard Rutherford. *The Rites of Death and Dying*, 1987 National Meeting of The Federation of Diocesan Liturgical Committees. Collegeville, MN: The Liturgical Press, 1988.

Catholic Conference of Canadian Bishops. "The Christian Funeral," *National Bulletin on Liturgy*, 22, No. 119 (197-257), December, 1989.

Curley, Terence P. *Console One Another: A Guide for Christian Funerals*. Kansas City, MO: Sheed & Ward, 1993.

_____. "Music Expressing Pastoral Care for the Bereaved," *Pastoral Life*. Vol. 41, No. 1 (21) January, 1992.

_____. "The Funeral Homily: Pastoral Care at a Critical Time," *Pastoral Life*. Vol. 41, No. 7 (27) July-August, 1992.

_____. "Saying Farewell During The Funeral," *The Priest*, Vol. 48, No. 8 (45) August, 1992.

_____. *A Way of the Cross for the Bereaved*. New York: Alba House, 1996.

Rutherford, H. Richard. "Homilies vs. Eulogies, Preaching at Catholic Funerals," *Modern Liturgy*, Vol. 19, No. 7 (10) 1992.

_____. *The Death of a Christian*. Collegeville, MN: The Liturgical Press, 1990.

Seig, Thomas H. "Preaching at Funerals: Homily or Eulogy?" *The Priest*, Vol. 40 (42) 1984.

Funeral Professionals

Curley, Terence P. "New Funeral Ritual Means Change for Funeral Directors," *American Funeral Director*, Vol. 114, No. 3 (24) March, 1991.

_____. "Separation and Loss," *American Funeral Director*, Vol. 114, No. 11 (36) November, 1991.

_____. "Religious Symbols Create A Supportive Atmosphere," *American Funeral Director*, Vol. 114, No. 8 (42) August, 1991.

_____. "Catholic Funeral Ritual Emphasizes Burial Service," *American Funeral Director*, Vol. 115, (38) No. 2. February, 1992.

Curley, Jerome M. & Terence P. "Recognizing the Symptoms of Stress and Burnout," *American Funeral Director*, (80) VI, 114, No. 10. October, 1991.

Curley, Terence P. *Journey to Healing: A Ministry for the Bereaved*, Canfield, OH: Alba House Communications. Four (4) thirty-minute presentations. The bereaved are invited to explore (1) The dynamics of grief, (2) needs facing them, (3) breaking open the Word and (4) contemporary understanding about loss. 1 (800) 343-2522. (Fax) 718-761-0057. In Canada 1 (800) 668-2078.